Instant Website Optimization for Retina Displays How-to

Learning simple techniques which will make your website look stunning on high-definition Retina Displays

Kyle J. Larson

BIRMINGHAM - MUMBAI

Instant Website Optimization for Retina Displays How-to

First published: January 2013

Production Reference: 1160113

Published by Packt Publishing Ltd.
Livery Place
35 Livery Street
Birmingham B3 2PB, UK.

ISBN 978-1-84969-512-1

www.packtpub.com

Credits

Author
Kyle J. Larson

Reviewer
Jan Rajtoral

IT Content Commissioning Editor
Grant Mizen

Commissioning Editor
Maria D'souza

Technical Editor
Worrell Lewis

Project Coordinator
Amigya Khurana

Proofreader
Aaron Nash

Production Coordinator
Prachali Bhiwandkar

Cover Work
Prachali Bhiwandkar

Cover Image
Sheetal Aute

About the Author

Kyle Larson is a self-taught web designer and front-end developer who has been passionate about the power of networks since he got his first modem at the age of 10. He studied art and design at the University of Minnesota while working for `http://www.techies.com/`, a job search start-up.

Kyle is currently a Senior Web Designer, designing for a variety of brands, at Milestone AV Technologies in Minnesota. He also does freelance work with Emergent Networks and a variety of small businesses. When he's not buried in a web project, Kyle blogs about what he learns at `http://www.kylejlarson.com/`.

I'd like to thank: My parents, Jim and Nancy, and my sister, Caitlin, for being the best family I could ask for and pretending to understand my technobabble. Steve and Barb for being fun and always supportive. Jessi for being all-around awesome and always understanding when my schedule gets crazy. My buddies Justin, Brian, Brandon, Danny, Andy, and Elliot for the great breaks from writing. Fore!

About the Reviewer

Jan Rajtoral, aka Gonzo the Great, is the founder of and designer at gonzodesign, a Dutch design studio providing design services across the full spectrum of graphic design and (responsive) web design.

He also writes for `http://www.gonzoblog.nl/`, where above everything else, his passion for writing, technology, communication, and design drives him to contribute.

www.PacktPub.com

Support files, eBooks, discount offers and more

You might want to visit www.PacktPub.com for support files and downloads related to your book.

Did you know that Packt offers eBook versions of every book published, with PDF and ePub files available? You can upgrade to the eBook version at www.PacktPub.com and as a print book customer, you are entitled to a discount on the eBook copy. Get in touch with us at service@packtpub.com for more details.

At www.PacktPub.com, you can also read a collection of free technical articles, sign up for a range of free newsletters and receive exclusive discounts and offers on Packt books and eBooks.

http://PacktLib.PacktPub.com

Do you need instant solutions to your IT questions? PacktLib is Packt's online digital book library. Here, you can access, read and search across Packt's entire library of books.

Why Subscribe?

- ▶ Fully searchable across every book published by Packt
- ▶ Copy and paste, print and bookmark content
- ▶ On demand and accessible via web browser

Free Access for Packt account holders

If you have an account with Packt at www.PacktPub.com, you can use this to access PacktLib today and view nine entirely free books. Simply use your login credentials for immediate access.

Table of Contents

Preface

Instant Website Optimization for Retina Displays How-to is a comprehensive guide to building a website that looks fantastic on high pixel density displays. Helpful insights and simple instructions walk you through all the various methods of optimizing your site for the latest mobile and desktop devices.

Apple launched its line of high pixel density, Retina Display products with the iPhone 4 and has continued to integrate the technology into its other products. A high pixel density display typically has one and a half to two times the amount of pixels per inch of a traditional display. This makes the pixels nearly invisible to the human eye. These beautiful displays take computing to a new level with incredibly sharp text and graphics.

Apple's marketing of the Retina brand popularized the high pixel density display, but the techniques in this book apply to many other manufacturers' devices with similar displays. As these displays become cheaper to manufacture, high-density graphics will become the new standard for the apps and websites of the future.

This book begins by covering the basics of Retina images and dives right into practical advice so you can start improving your website's images. It continues building on the basic techniques with simple recipes covering all the tools you'll need to make an impressive Retina website.

We will take a look at the techniques for adding Retina backgrounds, sprites, and border images. You will learn how to optimize your site, loading large images only when needed to keep it running fast. We will create a variety of basic shapes and styles using CSS that can be used instead of graphics in your user interface. We'll cover scalable image techniques, including using fonts as icons and implementing Scalable Vector Graphics (SVG), which make your graphics look great on any device.

After reading *Instant Website Optimization for Retina Displays How-to* you'll have mastered the techniques to make creating high-density websites easy.

What this book covers

Creating your first Retina image (Must know), will help you create a high-density image and implement it using the HTML <IMG> tag. You will also learn the importance of consistent file names.

Retina background images (Must know), teaches you to use CSS to add high-definition background images.

Optimizing (Must know), explains techniques for optimizing images, what tools are available, and why it matters for speed.

Creating image sprites (Should know), will help you use CSS to add high-definition image sprites that make fewer HTTP requests for increased speed.

CSS border images (Should know), will teach you to create high-definition border images in CSS.

CSS media queries (Should know), explains how media queries can determine when your new Retina images are loaded.

CSS image-set (Become an expert), will teach you a possible future technique for adding Retina images to your site.

Using code instead of images (Must know), explains how to use CSS3 to create resolution-independent graphical elements.

Embedding fonts (Should know), explains how fonts scale on Retina Devices and how they can be added to your site via embedding and font services.

Fonts as icons (Should know), helps you create graphics using fonts.

High-resolution web apps (Should know), helps you create high-quality, web-clip icons for mobile devices and favicons for the browser.

Scalable Vector Graphics (Become an expert), helps you create SVG as a replacement for images.

Canvas (Become an expert), explains how Canvas can be coded to adapt to high-density displays.

Pixel ratio detection with JavaScript (Become an expert), will teach you to use JavaScript to detect if a device has a high-density display and serve the correct image.

Server-side Retina solutions (Become an expert), explains how a server-side code can be used to detect if high-definition images should be served.

What you need for this book

You'll need to have a high-definition device to be able to test the examples in this book and a server to upload your code to if you're not developing it on that device. You'll need a graphics editor (such as Photoshop or GIMP) and a code editor (such as Coda, Dreamweaver, TextEdit, or Notepad).

Who this book is for

This book is for web designers and developers who are familiar with HTML, CSS, and graphics editing and would like to improve their existing website or their next web project with high-density images.

Conventions

In this book, you will find a number of styles of text that distinguish between different kinds of information. Here are some examples of these styles, and an explanation of their meaning.

Code words in text are shown as follows: "Make sure you enter the correct `background-size` dimensions for your image."

A block of code is set as follows:

```
<style>
   .imgHeader { width: 700px; height: 400px; }
</style>
<img src="images/myImage@2x.jpg" class="imgHeader" />
```

New terms and **important words** are shown in bold. Words that you see on the screen, in menus or dialog boxes for example, appear in the text like this: "Choose **Save for Web** or **Export...**".

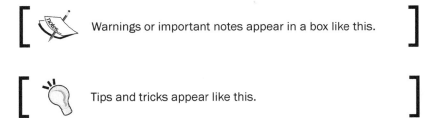

Warnings or important notes appear in a box like this.

Tips and tricks appear like this.

Reader feedback

Feedback from our readers is always welcome. Let us know what you think about this book—what you liked or may have disliked. Reader feedback is important for us to develop titles that you really get the most out of.

To send us general feedback, simply send an e-mail to `feedback@packtpub.com`, and mention the book title via the subject of your message.

If there is a topic that you have expertise in and you are interested in either writing or contributing to a book, see our author guide on `www.packtpub.com/authors`.

Customer support

Now that you are the proud owner of a Packt book, we have a number of things to help you to get the most from your purchase.

Downloading the example code

You can download the example code files for all Packt books you have purchased from your account at `http://www.PacktPub.com`. If you purchased this book elsewhere, you can visit `http://www.PacktPub.com/support` and register to have the files e-mailed directly to you.

Errata

Although we have taken every care to ensure the accuracy of our content, mistakes do happen. If you find a mistake in one of our books—maybe a mistake in the text or the code—we would be grateful if you would report this to us. By doing so, you can save other readers from frustration and help us improve subsequent versions of this book. If you find any errata, please report them by visiting `http://www.packtpub.com/support`, selecting your book, clicking on the **errata submission form** link, and entering the details of your errata. Once your errata are verified, your submission will be accepted and the errata will be uploaded on our website, or added to any list of existing errata, under the Errata section of that title. Any existing errata can be viewed by selecting your title from `http://www.packtpub.com/support`.

Piracy

Piracy of copyright material on the Internet is an ongoing problem across all media. At Packt, we take the protection of our copyright and licenses very seriously. If you come across any illegal copies of our works, in any form, on the Internet, please provide us with the location address or website name immediately so that we can pursue a remedy.

Please contact us at `copyright@packtpub.com` with a link to the suspected pirated material.

We appreciate your help in protecting our authors, and our ability to bring you valuable content.

Questions

You can contact us at `questions@packtpub.com` if you are having a problem with any aspect of the book, and we will do our best to address it.

Instant Website Optimization for Retina Displays How-to

Welcome to *Instant Website Optimization for Retina Displays How-to*. This book covers how to create images for the latest high-definition displays. Apple's Retina Display created a new standard in quality for imagery on the Web. Understanding the challenges presented by this new technology and learning the techniques in this book to overcome them will be essential to designing for the future web.

Creating your first Retina image (Must know)

Apple's Retina Display is a brand name for their high pixel density screens. These screens have so many pixels within a small space that the human eye cannot see pixelation, making images and text appear smoother. To compete with Apple's display, other manufacturers are also releasing devices using high-density displays. These types of displays are becoming standard in high quality devices.

When you first start browsing the Web using a Retina Display, you'll notice that many images on your favorite sites are blurry. This is a result of low-resolution images being stretched to fill the screen. The effect can make an otherwise beautiful website look unattractive.

The key to making your website look exceptional on Retina Displays is the quality of the images that you are using. In this recipe, we will cover the basics of creating high-resolution images and suggestions on how to name your files. Then we'll use some simple HTML to display the image on a web page.

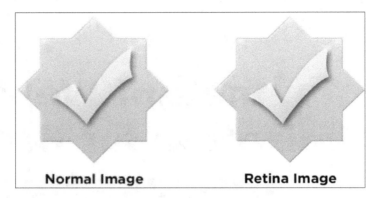

Normal Image   **Retina Image**

Getting ready

Creating a Retina-ready site doesn't require any special software beyond what you're already using to build web pages. You'll need a graphics editor (such as Photoshop or GIMP) and your preferred code/text editor. To test the code on Retina Display you'll also need a web server that you can reach from a browser, if you aren't coding directly on the Retina device.

The primary consideration in getting started is the quality of your images. A Retina image needs to be at least two times as large as it will be displayed on screen. If you have a photo you'd like to add to your page that is 500 pixels wide, you'll want to start out with an image that is at least 1000 pixels wide. Trying to increase the size of a small image won't work because the extra pixels are what make your image sharp.

When designing your own graphics, such as icons and buttons, it's best to create them using a vector graphics program so they will be easy to resize without affecting the quality. Once you have your high-resolution artwork gathered, we're ready to start creating Retina images.

How to do it...

1. To get started, let's create a folder on your computer called `retina`. Inside that folder, create another folder called `images`. We'll use this as the directory for building our test website.

2. To create your first Retina image, first open a high-resolution image in your graphics editor. You'll want to set the image size to be double the size of what you want to display on the page. For example, if you wanted to display a 700 x 400 pixel image, you would start with an image that is 1400 x 800 pixels. Make sure you aren't increasing the size of the original image or it won't work correctly.

3. Next, save this image as a `.jpg` file with the filename `myImage@2x.jpg` inside of the `/images/` folder within the `/retina/` folder that we created. Then resize the image to 50 percent and save it as `myImage.jpg` to the same location.

4. Now we're ready to add our new images to a web page. Create an HTML document called `retinaTest.html` inside the `/retina/` folder. Inside of the basic HTML structure add the two images we created and set the dimensions for both images to the size of the smaller image.

```
<body>
    <img src="images/myImage@2x.jpg" width="700" height="400" />
    <img src="images/myImage.jpg" width="700" height="400" />
</body>
```

5. If you are working on a Retina device you should be able to open this page locally; if not, upload the folder to your web server and open the page on your device. You will notice how much sharper the first image is than the second image. On a device without a Retina Display, both images will look the same. Congratulations! you've just built your first Retina-optimized web page.

How it works...

Retina Displays have a higher amount of **pixels per inch** (**PPI**) than a normal display. In Apple's devices they have double the PPI of older devices, which is why we created an image that was two times as large as the final image we wanted to display. When that large image is added to the code and then resized to 50 percent, it has more data than what is being shown on a normal display. A Retina device will see that extra pixel data and use it to fill the extra PPI that its screen, contains. Without the added pixel data, the device will use the data available to fill the screen creating a blurry image. You'll notice that this effect is most obvious on large photos and computer graphics like icons. Keep in mind this technique will work with any image format such as `.jpg`, `.png`, or `.gif`.

There's more...

As an alternative to using the image width and height attributes in HTML, like the previous code, you can also give the image a CSS class with width and height attributes. This is only recommended if you will be using many images that are of the same size and you want to be able to change them easily.

```
<style>
    .imgHeader { width: 700px; height: 400px; }
</style>
<img src="images/myImage@2x.jpg" class="imgHeader" />
```

Tips for creating images

We created both a Retina and a normal image. It's always a good idea to create both images because the Retina image will be quite a bit larger than the normal one. Then you'll have the option of which image you'd like to have displayed so users without a Retina device don't have to download the larger file.

You'll also notice that we added @2x to the filename of the larger image. It's a good practice to create consistent filenames to differentiate the images that are high-resolution. It'll make our coding work much easier going forward.

Pixels per inch and dots per inch

When designers with a print background first look into creating graphics for Retina Displays there can be some confusion regarding **dots per inch** (**DPI**). Keep in mind that computer displays are only concerned with the number of pixels in an image. An 800 x 600 pixel image at 300 DPI will display the same as an 800 x 600 pixel image at 72 DPI.

Retina background images (Must know)

When creating a website that is optimized for Retina Displays, you'll want to make sure that you are updating all the images on your site so everything looks sharp. In addition to updating your images in HTML, you'll also want to update any background images that you have set in CSS. Background images are often used to create the template that is used throughout a website, so they are critical in optimizing for Retina Displays.

How to do it...

1. We'll start working with background images by creating two versions of an image just like we did for regular images. If you don't already have a good background texture to use there are a lot of great options at `www.backgroundlabs.com`. In your graphics editor resize the image to double the size that you'd like a single tile to be and save the file in the `/images/` folder within the `/retina/` folder as `myBackground@2x.jpg`. For our example we'll use 250 x 150 pixels. Next, resize the image to 50 percent and save it as `myBackground.jpg` in the same folder.

2. Now let's add our background images to a web page to test them out. Create a new HTML document in your editor called `backgroundTest.html` and save it in the `/retina/` folder. First, we'll add our CSS code into the file (it is typically a good idea to create a separate CSS file but for the example we'll add it in our HTML page).

```
<style>
.box {
  height: 200px;
  width: 700px;
}
```

```
.bgRetina {
  background: url(images/myBackground@2x.jpg) repeat;
  background-size: 250px 150px;
}
.bgNormal {
  background: url(images/myBackground.jpg) repeat;
  background-size: 250px 150px;
}
</style>
```

3. This CSS code will create a box to display the background within and then apply our image to it. Make sure you enter the correct `background-size` dimensions for your image (based on the smaller of the two images). Next we'll add the HTML code as follows to our CSS:

```
<div class="box bgRetina">Retina</div>
<div class="box bgNormal">Normal</div>
```

4. Now we're ready to test out our Retina background. If you're on a Retina device load the page in your browser, otherwise copy the new files to your server and open them up in your browser. The first background will look much sharper on the Retina Display.

How it works...

The background image example works based on the same concept as creating a normal Retina image. You are filling an area with an image that contains double the amount of pixels needed for a normal display. The `background-size` property tells the browser what size each tile of the background should be. The same principles apply to all background images, even if they are not a repeating pattern.

There's more...

The `background-size` CSS property was added in CSS Version 3. This means it is not supported in older browsers such as Internet Explorer 7 and 8. In these browsers the background will be larger than intended, which is still functional but not ideal. To support these browsers, you'll want to only use Retina background images as part of a media query. We will cover this in more detail in the *CSS Media Queries* recipe.

Optimizing (Must know)

You may have noticed that the file sizes of Retina images are quite a bit larger than normal images. This is a point of concern, especially for mobile users. Although our data networks have rapidly increased in speed in recent years, it's still important to make sure our sites are optimized for slower connections.

There are a number of different techniques you can apply to make sure your images load quickly. This recipe will cover how to choose the best image format to use in various situations and how to use compression in several tools for images with smaller file sizes.

Getting ready

There are a number of image editing programs you can use to create graphics for the Web. In this recipe we'll cover using **Photoshop** and **GIMP** to edit images, but the principles should apply to most applications. If you do not have a good image-editing program that allows compression, GIMP is free to download at `http://www.gimp.org/`. If you'd like to optimize some images that you've already created there are some automatic compression tools available that we'll discuss as well.

Before you start trying to create optimized images, it's important to understand what file formats work best for various situations. The three main image formats you'll come across are **GIF**, **JPEG** (**JPG**), and **PNG**.

In most situations GIF is used for logos or low detail icons, JPEG is optimal for photos, and PNG is best for detailed graphics with transparency. Let's gather one image, that would work well for each scenario, to optimize.

How to do it...

1. To get started let's work on optimizing a PNG image. Open any high color photo or graphic. The first thing we will do is **posterize** the image. This will reduce the number of color variations that the image contains.

2. In Photoshop, go to **Image | Adjustments | Posterize...** in the menu bar. In GIMP go to **Tools | Color Tools | Posterize...**. This will open a dialog box allowing you to change the number of levels. Lowering the number will decrease the amount of colors used and reduce the size of the file. Start with a large number and slowly decrease it while watching the image preview. Find a level where the difference in the image isn't very noticeable.

3. Next save the image as a PNG (PNG-24) via **Export...** in GIMP or **Save for Web** in Photoshop. In GIMP you can leave the compression level at **9**.

4. Now we'll optimize a GIF image. Open a logo, clipart, or similar image file in your graphics editor. In Photoshop choose **File | Save for Web** and then select GIF as your image type. On the right-hand side you'll see a drop-down list for **Colors**. Decreasing this number will result in a smaller image by removing similar colors. If you find it is removing a color that you don't want, you can select that color in the pallet below and click on the lock icon. In GIMP from the menu bar select **Image | Mode | Indexed...**. Try choosing a maximum number of colors less than 255. Choose a low number of colors that still looks good (try somewhere around 128 first). You'll find that some GIFs compress well and others do not, based on the initial amount of colors.

5. Finally, we'll optimize a JPEG image. Open a photograph in your image editor. Choose **Save for Web** or **Export...**. Both GIMP and Photoshop will present a similar slider that will allow you to set the image quality. The more this number is reduced the more image data will be lost. Typically you can save an image somewhere between 70 percent and 80 percent without noticing much quality loss. When creating Retina images, you may find that you can compress some photos much more than a standard definition image and it still looks good in the browser. Experiment with these settings to see what works best. You can view the preview as you change the setting to see the final result.

How it works...

Each type of image works slightly differently and has a different method of compression. It's important to choose the optimal image format based on the contents of the image in relation to the strengths of each format.

GIF images are best for simple illustrations and icons because they support transparency but only display a maximum of 256 colors. They will compress well if you have large areas of the same color and use very few colors. In most cases, GIF will be your least used image type.

JPEG images are often used for photos because they support millions of colors and compress well. JPEGs are **lossy**, which means you can lower the quality of the image in exchange for a smaller file size. When compressing a JPEG it is a good idea to keep the original because, once compressed, the image data is gone. JPEGs do not allow transparency.

PNG images combine some of the benefits of GIFs and JPEGs. They work well for photos but are best suited for graphics with transparency. PNGs have high quality transparency without the jagged edge you may find in a GIF image and work better with many colors. They are based on a **lossless** compression, which retains the image data so you will not be able to compress photos as much as a JPEG.

When starting an optimization plan, it's best to start by focusing on images that most users will have to download. These include graphics that are used in your template and your most visited pages. You can also sort your site's images folder by size and optimize your largest images first. In some cases, you may find that your images can be compressed enough to serve only your Retina image without worrying about your site loading slowly. This is by far the simplest Retina solution. For an example of this, read Daan Jobsis' article at `http://blog.netvlies.nl/design-interactie/retina-revolution/`.

There's more...

In addition to being able to manually optimize your images, there are a number of tools that will automatically optimize images based on algorithms. These may not always be the most compressed an image could get, but when looking to save time this can be a better option.

There is a variety of software that will help you with compression, such as the following:

- ▶ TinyPNG – `http://tinypng.org/` (web-based)
- ▶ ImageOptim – `http://imageoptim.com/` (Mac)
- ▶ RIOT – `http://luci.criosweb.ro/riot/` (Windows)
- ▶ PNGGauntlet – `http://pnggauntlet.com/` (Windows)

Tips for creating repeating backgrounds

When using repeating background images, it is best to make the image the smallest possible tile. For example, a repeating grid pattern could be made with only two connected lines of a square. Try creating your graphic and placing a duplicate next to it to figure out the smallest portion of the pattern needed.

Creating image sprites (Should know)

When building a large website, it is important to minimize the amount of images that a user has to download. This lowers the amount of **HTTP requests** that the browser needs to make and improves the loading time. Image sprites help you accomplish this by combining a group of images into a single image.

Sprites are a great way to group sets of icons or other similar graphics that are used in your template. If you are creating an interface for a bank, you may have icons for search, savings, checking, loans, advice, and more. Instead of saving these files individually, you can group them into a sprite to speed up the download.

In this recipe, we'll explain how to create an image sprite and how to make a Retina version. Then we'll add both versions to a test page using HTML and CSS.

Getting ready

To get started you'll want to gather four icons that are of the same size in your graphics editor. Look for icons that are large because your Retina image sprite will need to be 2x as large as the icons are displayed on screen. For our example, we'll be using icons that are 80 x 80 pixels.

How to do it...

1. First take the four images that you've collected and make sure that they are of the same size. Then create a new image that is 2x as tall and 2x as wide as each image (for 80 x 80 icons the new image would be 160 x 160). Place each icon in a quadrant of the new image so they fill the space. Save this image as a PNG inside the /images/ folder within the /retina/ folder with the filename `mySprite@2x.png`. Then resize the image to 50 percent and save it as `mySprite.png` in the same folder.

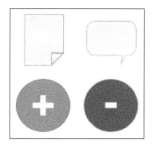

2. Now we'll test the two versions of the sprites on a web page. Create an HTML document called `spritesTest.html` inside the `/retina/` folder. Next, we'll add some CSS code to the basic HTML structure, using the measurements of a single one of your non-Retina icons (40 x 40 for this example). The background-size attribute should equal the full size of your small, non-Retina, sprite.

```
<style>

.icon {
  background: url(images/mysprite.png);
  height: 40px;
  width: 40px;
}
.iconRetina {
  background: url(images/mysprite@2x.png);
  background-size: 80px 80px;
  height: 40px;
  width: 40px;
}
.icon1 {background-position: 0 0;}
.icon2 {background-position: -40px 0;}
.icon3 {background-position: 0 -40px;}
.icon4 {background-position: -40px -40px;}

</style>
```

3. This CSS code will let us set either regular or Retina icons depending on the class that we use. Now we'll add in the HTML code to display both the sprites so that we can compare them.

```
<ul>
  <li class="icon icon1"></li>
  <li class="iconRetina icon2"></li>
  <li class="icon icon3"></li>
  <li class="iconRetina icon4"></li>
</ul>
```

4. If you are working on a Retina device you will be able to open this page locally; if not, upload the folder to your web server and open the page on your device. You will notice that icons 2 and 4 are much sharper than icons 1 and 3.

How it works...

Image sprites are large images that contain multiple smaller images. This image is then set to the background of an HTML element with a height and width equal to only one of the images in the sprite. This prevents all the images in the sprite from being displayed.

To determine which image in the sprite is displayed, `background-position` is changed. The first value of `background-position` is the **X value** and the second is the **Y value**. A negative X value slides the image to the left-hand side and a negative Y value slides the image up. To figure out the correct offset, count the number of pixels from the top-left corner (which is `0, 0`) of your image to where the icon you'd like to display begins. Note that when any value in CSS is `0` you don't need to include `px`.

The Retina sprite works the same way, but the image is twice as large. To compensate for this difference, we set the `background-size` property to the dimensions of the smaller image. Now we have twice as many pixels inside of the same space for the Retina Display to create a sharp image.

There's more...

The `background-size` CSS property was added in CSS Version 3. This means it is not supported in older browsers such as Internet Explorer 7 and 8. In these browsers the background will be larger than intended, which is not ideal. To support these browsers, you'll want to only use Retina background images as part of a media query. We will cover this in more detail in the CSS Media Queries recipe.

Tips for creating image sprites

In our example we created an image sprite with four icons that were of the same size. This was only done for simplicity. When you create an image sprite for your website you can include images of all sizes. You might have two different sized sets of icons, a logo, graphics for a navigation menu, or backgrounds for tabs. When creating the sprite, it will save you time if you group similar sized images together so it will be easier to figure out the measurements for your CSS code.

CSS border images (Should know)

Border images were introduced in CSS3 and are not widely used yet. This topic has been included in case you'd like to experiment with border images, but be aware that they are not supported in Internet Explorer. To find more about CSS support in various browsers take a look at http://caniuse.com/. Border images allow you to wrap a border around an HTML element using CSS and an image instead of the standard dotted, dashed, or solid line border. This can be especially useful when applying a border to a group of images or calling out specific content. This recipe will cover how to turn your border images into high-resolution Retina images.

Getting ready

To get started we'll need to gather a couple of images. First, get a high quality image you'd like to use as a border. It should be a full square and could be a picture frame, torn paper, or some other repeating pattern. For our demo we'll be placing the border on an image, and any photo will work. After you've gathered these two graphics we're ready to build a Retina border image.

How to do it...

1. First, open the border image you chose in your graphics editor. Just like other Retina images, you'll want the initial graphic to be 2x as large as it will be displayed on screen. Save this image as myBorder@2x.png into the /images/ folder that is within the /retina/ folder. Then resize the image to 50 percent and save it as myBorder.png into the same folder.

2. Next save the photo you've selected into the `/images/` folder within the `/retina/` folder as `myBorderPhoto.jpg`. Now we've got all the images ready to start writing our CSS and HTML code.

3. Create a new HTML document called `borderTest.html` inside of the `/retina/` folder. Add some CSS to create the border.

```
<style>

.imageBorder {
  border-width: 10px;
  -webkit-border-image: url(images/myBorder.png) 10 repeat;
  border-image: url(images/myBorder.png) 10 repeat;
}

.imageBorderRetina {
  border-width: 10px;
  -webkit-border-image: url(images/myBorder@2x.png) 10 repeat;
  border-image: url(images/myBorder@2x.png) 20 repeat;
}

</style>
```

4. Then add your photo in HTML and apply the CSS styles to create both a Retina and non-Retina border image.

```
<img class="imageBorder" src="images/myBorderPhoto.jpg />
<img class="imageBorderRetina" src="images/myBorderPhoto.jpg />
```

5. If you are working on a Retina device you will be able to open this page locally; if not, upload the folder to your web server and open the page on your device. You'll notice that the second border is much sharper than the first.

How it works...

To create our border, first we set the `border-width` property in CSS to specify how wide the border will be on each side of our image. If we wanted different widths, we could list out each side starting at the top and continuing clockwise, ending on the left-hand side (for example, `border-width: 5px 10px 15px 5px;`).

Next we add in two `border-image` statements to create the border. The first includes the `-webkit` vendor prefix, which allows the code to work in older versions of iOS. The first part of the property sets the image URL. The following numerical value tells the browser where to slice the image. You can include a value for each side of the border just like the `border-width` property. We've used pixels, but this can also be a percentage. The final value in the property determines the method of generating the border (`repeat`, `round`, or `stretch`).

The trick to getting the Retina border to work is doubling the slice value. This is because the Retina image is twice as large as the original and has double the pixels. If you were using a percentage value instead of pixels you would leave the value the same for each border image.

CSS media queries (Should know)

Making all devices download large Retina images, even if they cannot display them, is not deal. Doing this makes users wait longer to view your content without any benefit. Using **media queries** in your CSS is one way to get around this issue.

Media queries check to see if the user's device meets specific conditions, and if not, supply an alternate style. These are particularly useful in adjusting your website to a specific media, screen size, device orientation, or display type.

t is recommended that you use a media query or other image replacement technique every time you're using Retina images rather than only supplying a large image. Media queries will help accomplish this for any images that are contained within your CSS, such as backgrounds, image sprites, and border images. This recipe will explain how media queries can be used for each of these images to target only Retina Displays.

Getting ready

To build our media queries we'll be using the images that we have previously created. These nclude a Retina and normal version of a background image, an image sprite, and a border mage with a photo to wrap it around.

How to do it...

1. To get started, create a new HTML document called `mediaQueries.html` inside the `/retina/` folder. Then inside of the basic HTML structure we'll add the non-Retina CSS code for a background image, an image sprite, and a border.

2. First, we'll add a `box` style to hold our background image and the non-Retina version of the background image code.

```
<style>

.box {
height: 200px;
width: 700px;
}

.background {
background: url(images/myBackground.jpg) repeat;
}
```

3. Then we'll add the CSS code for our non-Retina image sprite.

```
.icon {
background: url(images/mysprite.png);
height: 40px;
width: 40px;
}
```

4. Next we'll add the code for a non-Retina border image.

```
.imageBorder {
border-width: 10px;
-webkit-border-image: url(images/myBorder.png) 10 repeat;
border-image: url(images/myBorder.png) 10 repeat;
}
```

5. Now we're ready to add a media query that will replace these images if the user is on a Retina Display.

```
@media
only screen and (-webkit-min-device-pixel-ratio: 2),
only screen and (min-device-pixel-ratio: 2) {

  .background {
    background: url(images/myBackground@2x.jpg) repeat;
    background-size: 250px 150px;
    }

  .icon {
    background: url(images/mysprite@2x.png);
    background-size: 80px 80px;
}
  .imageBorder {
    -webkit-border-image: url(images/myBorder@2x.png) 20 repeat;
    border-image: url(images/myBorder@2x.png) 20 repeat;


  }
} /* END OF MEDIA QUERY */
To complete the CSS, we'll add the styles to position our icons
and the closing style tag.
  .icon1 {background-position: 0 0;}
  .icon2 {background-position: -40px 0;}
  .icon3 {background-position: 0 -40px;}
  .icon4 {background-position: -40px -40px;}

</style>
```

6. To finish our code we'll just need to add some HTML to display our three types of images.

```
<div class="box background"></div>

<ul>
    <li class="icon icon1"></li>
    <li class="iconRetina icon2"></li>
    <li class="icon icon3"></li>
    <li class="iconRetina icon4"></li>
</ul>

<img class="imageBorder" src="images/myImage.jpg" />
```

How it works...

To use a media query in our CSS, first we created all the code we would need for our non-Retina images. After that we created the media query statement. The order is important because CSS is cascading, meaning that code is read top to bottom. If the media query preceded the other code, its rules would be overwritten by the code following it.

Our media query is composed of four parts. First, `@media` begins the media query statement. Then `only screen` specifies that the device being used must be a screen (another media type could be print). Next, we specify that the `min-device-pixel-ratio` must be equal to or greater than two. This targets the Retina Display (or any other similar display) because it has a pixel density that is two times greater than a standard display (some other devices use a ratio of 1.5). We also included the `-webkit` vendor prefix to make sure that our code works on older Safari browsers. To keep our code short we only included one vendor prefix, but if you want full support you may need other prefixes (`-o`, `-ms`, `-moz`). You can find out more about browser support at `http://caniuse.com/`. Finally, the brackets will enclose any style that we would like applied if these conditions are met.

When we write our styles within the media query we will be overwriting the code written previously, replacing a normal image with a Retina one. Any property that we don't specifically overwrite will remain from the above code. Each type of image has some specific considerations.

To create a background image, we overwrote our image file location with the `@2x` version. Then we set `background-size` to scale the large image down to the same size as the normal one. This allows the extra pixels to fill the Retina Display.

Creating an image sprite is similar to the background image. We first overwrite the image with the high-resolution version and then set the `background-size` to shrink it back down. Note that we didn't need to set the `height` and `width` because the values used above are still correct. Each icon in the sprite needs to have its own positioning so the browser knows what part of the image to display. These `background-position` values need to be stated after the end of the media query, otherwise they will be overwritten and you will only see the top-left part of the image.

To add a Retina border, first we overwrite the image with a `@2x` version. Then we need to double the amount of pixels we are slicing. If you are using percentages you don't need to adjust the value. Also note that we're using the same `border-width` property so it doesn't need to be included in the media query.

You'll find that media queries are a good solution when you have only a few specific images that you need to replace. On large sites with many images you'll want to use one of the other Retina solutions described in this book.

There's more...

Media queries can also be used to target specific screen sizes or device types. For example, to target a small screen you could use the code `@media screen and (max-width: 480px)`. This can be used to have your site adapt well to a variety of screen sizes. This technique is called responsive web design, and it is a great alternative to creating different sites for mobile and desktop users. For more information on this topic, I recommend reading Ethan Marcotte's article on responsive web design at `http://www.alistapart.com/articles/responsive-web-design/`.

CSS image-set (Become an expert)

In **Safari 6** (included in **iOS 6**) Apple added a new method of adding Retina images to websites. The new `image-set` specification is an alternative to using media queries that makes formatting easier and allows for potential future benefits. This recipe is only for experimental use, as it will only work in new versions of Chrome and Safari.

The immediate benefit of using `image-set` is that the two images are listed next to each other in your CSS code, making it easier to read and update. The potential future benefit is that, according to the specification, the browser is able to make the decision about which image should be displayed. Once it is fully implemented in browsers, the browser may choose the lower resolution image in cases where there is a slow connection, or the user could specify which images they prefer.

The `image-set` specification works with image sprites and background images. This recipe will cover how to use the `image-set` property to provide the browser with image resolution options for background images.

Getting ready

To get started we'll be using the Retina and standard resolution background images we created in the *Retina background images* recipe. You'll need a large Retina background pattern and one half its size.

How to do it...

1. First, we'll create an HTML document called `imagesetTest.html` inside the `/retina/` folder to test our images. Inside of the basic HTML structure, add the CSS code to create a box and backgrounds to apply to it.

```
<style>

.box {
  height: 200px;
  width: 700px;
}

  .background {
  background: url(images/myBackground.jpg);
  background: -webkit-image-set(url(images/myBackground.jpg) 1x,
url(images/myBackground@2x.jpg) 2x);
}

.backgroundNormal {
  background: url(images/myBackground.jpg);
}

</style>
```

2. Then create some `div` tags in HTML with your two backgrounds to test them out.

```
<div class="box backgroundNormal" />
<div class="box background" />
```

3. If you are working on a Retina device (running Safari 6+, Chrome 21+, or another browser with `image-set` support) you will be able to open this page locally; if not, upload the folder to your web server and open the page on your device. You'll notice that the second background is much sharper than the first.

How it works...

To test out the CSS `image-set`, we first used a `div` tag with a set `height` and `width` to hold our background image. Then we applied a normal `background` property with a single image. This was created as a fallback for browsers that do not support the `image-set` property.

Then we added a second `background` property with `-webkit-image-set()` wrapping our two images. We used the `-webkit` browser prefix because `image-set` has not been finalized yet. This way we avoid any potential issue that could arise if there are changes to the final specification when it is released.

Within the `image-set` tag, we add the normal URL structure for both our background images separated by a comma. After each URL we include a value to specify the density of each image, the first being 1x and the Retina image being 2x.

Notice that when using this specification you don't need to include the `background-size` property that was necessary for other Retina background images.

There's more...

It's very important to keep in mind that the CSS `image-set` specification has not been finalized yet, and this code will not work on every high-definition device. I felt that it was important to include it here because, once the final version is agreed upon, this could be the preferred method of implementing Retina images in the future. It is recommended only for testing or if you feel that a high percentage of your users have upgraded their browsers and it is fine to allow others to see the standard resolution images.

Speed detection

The `image-set` specification leaves the choice of which image to display to the browser, which means that a variety of factors including connection speed could be used in the future to make this decision. Currently, connection speed isn't taken into account for any of these Retina solutions, but there are some projects that are experimenting with this approach. If you'd like to experiment with these projects you can check out Nathan Ford's pngy (`http://github.com/nathanford/pngy`) or Yahoo's boomerang (`http://yahoo.github.com/boomerang/doc`).

Using code instead of images (Must know)

Finding images that can be replaced with code accomplishes two goals at the same time. It will make your site load faster, and any graphics created using CSS will be high-definition. CSS3 introduced many new properties that can be used to create simple shapes and apply effects to elements and text.

When these CSS styles are applied they will fill all the pixels that are available on your device, so you don't need to worry about creating Retina versions. The code remains the same for all devices, which saves development time and loads quickly for your users. In this recipe we'll create a button and a few shapes using only code to demonstrate the different methods that can be used to create graphics with CSS.

How to do it...

1. To get started, create a new HTML document called `cssGraphics.html` inside the `/retina/` folder. Then inside the basic HTML structure we'll add some CSS code to create a button.

```
<style>

    .buttonArea {
      margin: 50px;
    }


    .button {
    background: #7999ff;
    background: -webkit-linear-gradient(#7999ff 0%, #002c62 100%);
    background: linear-gradient(#7999ff 0%, #002c62 100%);
    border-radius: 60px;
    box-shadow: 1px 1px 4px #666;
    cursor: pointer;
    padding: 10px 40px;
    color: #fff;
    font-size: 20px;
    text-align: center;
    text-decoration: none;
    text-shadow: 1px 1px 2px #000;
    }
```

2. Then we'll create a diamond for our first CSS shape.

```
.diamond {
  background: #000;
  margin: 40px 20px;
  width: 50px;
  height: 50px;
  -webkit-transform: rotate(45deg);
  transform: rotate(45deg);
}
```

3. Next we'll create a circle with CSS.

```
.circle {
  margin: 20px;
  background: #000;
  border-radius: 50px;
  width: 50px;
  height: 50px;
}
```

4. Finally, we'll create a triangle in CSS.

```
.triangle {
  margin: 20px;
  width: 0;
  height: 0;
  border-bottom: 25px solid transparent;
  border-top: 25px solid transparent;
  border-left: 25px solid #000;
}
</style>
```

5. Then we'll add the HTML code to display the button and shapes we created.

```
<div class="buttonArea">

  <a class="button">Click Me</a>

</div>

<div class="diamond"></div>

<div class="circle"></div>

<div class="triangle"></div>
```

6. If you run this code in your Retina device you should see all the elements we just created. Note that for our example we only added a vendor prefix for Webkit (Safari and Chrome). You'll need to add other browsers' vendor prefixes for additional support.

How it works...

The first element we created in our CSS code was the button. We started out by creating an optional wrapper called `buttonArea`, just to give the button some spacing so that it would look better in the browser. The button itself starts out with a few `background` settings. The first is a fallback for browsers that don't support gradients. Then we added a couple of background properties with `linear-gradients`. The first one includes the `-webkit` vendor prefix for browser support since this property isn't finalized at this point, although it is included in most new browsers. To support additional browsers, you'll also want to include their **vendor prefixes** (`-o, -moz, -ms`).

`linear-gradient` works by setting a color and its location. 0 percent is the color at the top of the button and 100 percent is the color at the bottom. This simple gradient will create a transition between these two colors. If you'd like to, you can create complex gradients with multiple values and also change the direction. You can find CSS gradient generators online that will help you when writing this code.

Next, we added the `border-radius` property to round the edges of the button. Changing this value will affect the amount of curve, letting you create rounded corners or a fully rounded edge like we did in this example.

The `box-shadow` property creates a drop-shadow on the element. The values for this property from left to right are the horizontal offset, the vertical offset, the blur radius, and the color. The first two properties change the distance of the shadow from your element, and the blur radius will determine how sharp your shadow appears. To create a shadow inside of your shape you can add `inset` before your other properties (`box-shadow: inset 1px 1px 4px #666`).

The next two elements were added to finish off the last details of our button. The `cursor` property makes sure that the button looks clickable when the user hovers over it, and the `padding` gives us some space between our text and the edges of the button.

The remaining styles in our button are to format the text. The main property to note here is `text-shadow`. This works the same as the `box-shadow` property by setting the offsets, blur, and color of the shadow.

Next we created a few shapes using CSS. We've added the `margin` values to the shapes to space them apart from each other. The diamond was built using a square and then rotating it with `transform`. Transforming uses a rotation value to move the element on its axis (`360` being a full circle). When using this property, you'll want to include vendor prefixes to include support for all browsers as this property is not finalized yet.

To create a circle we created a rectangle and then gave it `border-radius`. For this to work the radius value must be the same as the sides of the square.

To create our triangle we're making a box with no width or height and using borders to create the shape. Make the two perpendicular sides to the direction you want the arrow to point transparent. This will create the angle and then apply a border to the opposite direction to fill it in. You can also apply the `transform` property to point the triangle any direction.

There's more...

Now that you know how to create these different shapes you can try applying the effects we used on the button to enhance them. For example, you could use a shadow on a circle to create a callout on a product, or a gradient on an arrow to indicate a drop-down navigation element.

Transparencies

When creating shapes you may want to position them on top of each other to create a larger graphic. You can do this using the CSS `position` property. You can also add transparency to your shapes to reveal what is beneath them. To do this, you can use the `rgba` settings for your background (`background: rgba(255, 0, 0, 0.5);`). The first three values are the red, green, and blue color values followed by the alpha value (from 0 to 1). If you'd like the transparency to apply to the element and all of its children, you could use the `opacity` property instead (`opacity: 0.5;`).

CSS button effects

When you create a CSS button it's also worth noting that you can use the same hover effects you're used to using on other CSS links (`a:hover {}`). For example, you could change the gradient and shadow to make it look like the button is raising or lowering when the user hovers over it.

Embedding fonts (Should know)

Typography can be a powerful design tool when used well. A lack of options in typography on the Web used to force designers to use images for titles (or implement complicated alternatives). The issue with this approach is that it requires time to download the image and it can impair usability. In modern web design this problem can be solved using **web fonts** or **font services**, and best of all they automatically adapt to high-definition displays.

To add CSS web fonts, `@font-face` is used. It has been around for a while now, but the drawback has always been a lack of browser support for various font formats. These options include `.eot`, `.otf`, `.ttf`, and `.woff`. **Web Open Font Format** (**WOFF**) is the latest standard that has been adopted by most font foundries and web browsers. WOFF will likely be the primary format in the future. This recipe will cover how to add a web font to your page that includes support for older browsers and then we'll discuss **font services**.

Getting ready

To get started we'll need a font to work with. You shouldn't just use any font you may have on your computer, as it may not be permitted for use on the Web. If you have specific fonts you'd like to use, it's best to check with the foundry and see if it's available as a web font. For this example we'll use `http://www.fontsquirrel.com/` to select a free font kit with all the formats needed for full browser support.

Go to `http://fontsquirrel.com/fontface` to find a font kit that you'd like to use. These kits include all the formats that you'll need and a code sample of how to implement them. Alternatively, you could use their @font-face generator tool to create a kit from a font that you upload. For this example I've chosen to use the font **Bevan** within the **slab serif** section. Download the font kit and unzip the files.

How to do it...

1. To get started, move the `.eot`, `.svg`, `.ttf`, and `.woff` fonts that you downloaded, into your `/retina/` folder. Then create a new HTML document called `cssFonts.html` inside the `/retina/` folder. Within the basic HTML structure we'll add our CSS code to include our web font.

    ```
    <style>

        @font-face {
    ```

```css
    font-family: 'BevanRegular';
    src: url('Bevan-webfont.eot');
    src: url('Bevan-webfont.eot?#iefix') format('embedded-
opentype'),
         url('Bevan-webfont.woff') format('woff'),
         url('Bevan-webfont.ttf') format('truetype'),
         url('Bevan-webfont.svg#BevanRegular') format('svg');
}
```

2. Then we'll add a class to display our new font as a large header.

```css
.largeHeader {
    font-size: 40px;
    font-family: 'BevanRegular', Arial, sans-serif;
    font-weight: normal;
}
```

3. Next we'll add a final class for a small header.

```css
.smallHeader {
    font-size: 22px;
    font-family: 'BevanRegular', Arial, sans-serif;
    font-weight: normal;
}
```

```html
</style>
```

4. Then we'll add the HTML code to display our new headers.

```html
<h1 class="largeHeader">Our New Large Header</h1>

<h2 class="smallHeader">This header isn't as large</h2>
```

5. If you run this code inside of your browser you should see the new fonts. Notice that the text looks just as sharp on a Retina device.

How it works...

The `@font-face` tag allows us to define a font that we can use in our styles. The first property, font-family, creates a name to use for the font that we're going to define. Next we code the locations of the font files we're going to use. The initial `src` is for compatibility with old browsers. Then in the second `src` property we list out all the different formats for compatibility with as many browsers as possible. Browsers will take whichever font format they are able to display.

Next we create styles to apply to our header tags. To begin our `font-family` property we list our new font, `BevanRegular`, which we named in the `@font-face` statement. Make sure you wrap the name within quotes. Then you can list additional fonts as fallbacks in case the browser isn't able to understand the fonts we provided.

There's more...

Instead of having to find font packages online or deal with purchasing and converting fonts, you can use a **font service**. Font services host a variety of fonts on their servers and allow you to use them, for a fee or for free, by adding some JavaScript and CSS to your site. These services also take care of updating fonts, having versions available for different browsers, and licensing.

The disadvantage of using these services is that you're unable to host them on your own servers so there is a possibility of downtime. The advantages and convenience may outweigh this minor concern.

If you are interested in trying a font service, there are many to choose from. Some of the most popular services include `https://typekit.com/`, `http://www.google.com/webfonts`, and `http://fontdeck.com/`. These services all have different font options and different price models, so it's worth checking a few out to find the right fit for your site.

Fonts as icons (Should know)

Web fonts are typically used for applying different typefaces to your designs, but they can also be used to add high-definition icons. Typefaces that are made up of symbols and shapes are called **dingbats**. You may be familiar with some of these fonts that have been pre-installed on your computer, but typically they don't serve much purpose.

Web designers can find useful sets of dingbats that are specifically tailored for building websites. These include icons for social media, shopping carts, e-mail, zoom, print, and other images that are useful for designing user interfaces. You could even create your own font with custom icons for your site. In this recipe, we'll use what we learned in the embedding fonts recipe to add a dingbat font and create an RSS button.

Getting ready

To get started we need a dingbat font to work with. For this example, we'll be using the Modern Pictograms @font-face kit, which can be downloaded from `http://www.fontsquirrel.com/fonts/modern-pictograms`. Download the kit with all the font formats available to ensure compatibility with older browsers.

How to do it...

1. To get started, move the `.eot`, `.svg`, `.ttf`, and `.woff` fonts that you downloaded, into your `/retina/` folder. Then create a new HTML document called `dingbats.html` inside the `/retina/` folder. Within the basic HTML structure we'll add some CSS code to include our web font.

```
<style>

  @font-face {
    font-family: 'ModernPictogramsNormal';
    src: url('modernpics-webfont.eot');
    src: url('modernpics-webfont.eot?#iefix') format('embedded-
opentype'),
         url('modernpics-webfont.woff') format('woff'),
         url('modernpics-webfont.ttf') format('truetype'),
         url('modernpics-webfont.svg#ModernPictogramsNormal')
format('svg');
  }
```

2. Then we'll add a class that lets us create an RSS button.

```
.rssButton {
    background: #ff9c00;
    border-radius: 8px;
    cursor: pointer;
    height: 50px;
    width: 50px;
    margin: 20px;
    font-family:'ModernPictogramsNormal';
    font-size: 50px;
    color: #fff;
    line-height: 15px;
    text-align: center;
  }

</style>
```

3. Then we'll add the HTML code to display our button. The RSS icon is a "**^**" character, which is *Shift + 6* on the keyboard.

   ```
   <div class="rssButton">^</div>
   ```

4. If you run this code inside of your browser you should see the RSS button. Notice that the button is just as sharp on a Retina device while zooming in.

How it works...

To start creating our RSS icon we set up `@font-face` rules for the font kit we downloaded (refer to the previous recipe on embedding fonts for additional information). Then we created a class to format the button. We started out by creating the structure with an orange background, rounded corners, width, and height.

Next, we added the settings for our new dingbat font. I've added a `line-height` attribute here to make sure the icon is set in the middle of the button. Finally, we created a `div` with the `rssButton` class and added the ^ character to it, which is the RSS icon dingbat.

There's more...

The benefit of using a font instead of an image is that fonts are vector graphics. This means that the font will scale to any size because it is based on code rather than pixels. A user can zoom to any level on their device and the icon will still appear sharp. You can also reuse this icon at any size or color on your site without having to worry about creating additional images.

High-resolution web apps (Should know)

When creating web apps you'll want to provide icons and startup images for users that save your app to their home screen. If you don't add these icons your site will just be represented by a screenshot, which is not ideal. When dealing with Retina device icons we can also upgrade our **favicon**, which is displayed in your browser tab next to the page title. This recipe will show you how to add Retina favicons, app icons, and startup images to your site.

Getting ready

To get started we'll need to create a few graphics. Within your graphics editor, create a 32 x 32 pixel image for your favicon. This is typically a logo or an image that you feel represents your site.

Next create an app icon that is square and at least 144 x 144 pixels. A vector graphic is ideal for this icon so you can easily resize it without having to worry about the image quality. You have the option of rounding the corners of the icon yourself, or you can let the device round the corners for you. For this example we'll round the icon ourselves.

The corner radius of your rounded square should be 25.263 pixels to match Apple's icon styles. The formula to figure out the radius for any icon size is: *10/57 x icon size = radius*. There are also a number of iOS icon templates that can be found online to help you get started.

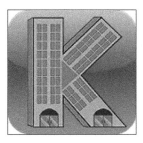

Finally, create a startup image at 1536 x 2048 pixels. This image will be used for iPad and iPhone and needs to be resized, so working with vector art is ideal. This image will be displayed when the user launches your site, if you allow it to be run as a web app.

How to do it...

1. Adding a Retina favicon is quick and simple, so we'll start with that. To add a high-definition favicon you'll just need to save your 32 x 32 image as an `.ico` file. If your graphics editor doesn't let you save in that format then save it as a PNG instead. You can find tools online to convert the file from PNG to ICO, such as `http://www.icoconverter.com/`. Put the `favicon.ico` file in the root directory of your site.

2. Next save your app icon as four PNG files in the `/retina/` folder with the following sizes and names:

   - 144 x 144 pixels – `apple-touch-icon-144x144-precomposed.png`
   - 114 x 114 pixels – `apple-touch-icon-114x114-precomposed.png`
   - 72 x 72 pixels – `apple-touch-icon-72x72-precomposed.png`
   - 57 x 57 pixels – `apple-touch-icon-precomposed.png`

3. After you've created all four app icons, create a new HTML document called `appIcons.html` inside the `/retina/` folder. Within the `<head>` tag of the basic HTML structure we'll add the code to run as a web app.

   ```
   <head>
     <meta name="apple-mobile-web-app-capable" content="yes" />
   ```

4. Next within the `<head>` tag we'll add the code for each of these icons.

   ```
   <link rel="apple-touch-icon-precomposed" href="apple-touch-icon-
   precomposed.png" />

   <link rel="apple-touch-icon-precomposed" sizes="72x72"
   href="apple-touch-icon-72x72-precomposed.png" />
   ```

```
<link rel="apple-touch-icon-precomposed" sizes="114x114"
href="apple-touch-icon-114x114-precomposed.png" />

<link rel="apple-touch-icon-precomposed" sizes="144x144"
href="apple-touch-icon-144x144-precomposed.png" />
```

5. Then we'll add your startup images. Save your startup image as seven different PNG files inside the `/retina/` folder with the following sizes and names:

    ❑   1536 x 2008 pixels – `apple-touch-startup-image-1536x2008.png`

    ❑   2048 x 1496 pixels (landscape) – `apple-touch-startup-image-`
        `1496x2048.png` (rotate this image 90 degrees clockwise before saving)

    ❑   768 x 1004 pixels – `apple-touch-startup-image-768x1004.png`

    ❑   1024 x 748 pixels (landscape) – `apple-touch-startup-image-`
        `748x1024.png` (rotate this image 90 degrees clockwise before saving)

    ❑   640 x 1096 pixels – `apple-touch-startup-image-640x1096.png`

    ❑   640 x 920 pixels – `apple-touch-startup-image@2x.png`

    ❑   320 x 460 pixels – `apple-touch-startup-image.png`

6. Now we'll add the code inside the `<head>` tag to display our startup images.

```
<link href="apple-touch-startup-image.png" media="(device-width:
320px)" rel="apple-touch-startup-image">

<link href="apple-touch-startup-image@2x.png" media="(device-
width: 320px) and (-webkit-device-pixel-ratio: 2)" rel="apple-
touch-startup-image">

<link href="apple-touch-startup-image@2x.png" media="(device-
width: 320px) and (device-height: 568px) and (-webkit-device-
pixel-ratio: 2)" rel="apple-touch-startup-image">

<link href="apple-touch-startup-image-768x1004.png"
media="(device-width: 768px) and (orientation: portrait)"
rel="apple-touch-startup-image">

<link href="apple-touch-startup-image-748x1024.png"
media="(device-width: 768px) and (orientation: landscape)"
rel="apple-touch-startup-image">

<link href="apple-touch-startup-image-1536x2008.png"
media="(device-width: 768px) and (orientation: portrait) and
(-webkit-device-pixel-ratio: 2)" rel="apple-touch-startup-image">
```

```
<link href="apple-touch-startup-image-1496x2048.png"
media="(device-width: 768px) and (orientation: landscape) and
(-webkit-device-pixel-ratio: 2)" rel="apple-touch-startup-image">

</head>
```

7. Finally we'll add a paragraph after the `<head>` tag so that our website has some content.

```
<p>Testing out some app icons</p>
```

8. If you open this page on your device and save it to your home screen as an app (in the Safari browser in your mobile press the box and arrow icon) you'll see the icon and startup image displayed.

How it works...

The first item we created was a favicon to show in bookmarks and the browser title. Normally favicons are 16 x 16 pixel files named `favicon.ico` that are uploaded to the root directory of your site. The Retina ICO file is double the amount of pixels. Browsers will automatically look for this filename within the root directory of your site.

Next we set up our site to run as a web app and gave it the necessary images. The `apple-mobile-web-app-capable` value for the `<meta>` tag tells the device that your site can function in full screen. If you're going to use this setting make sure you have all the appropriate navigation built in so the user doesn't need the back button. When the web app is saved to the home screen it will use the images that we specified in our code.

The first set of images we added create an app icon for our site. The browser will take the largest of these icons that it is able to display. These icons accommodate both iPhone and iPad screens. By including these in your code you can provide any filename for the images or location. If you save them with the filenames we used and save them in the root directory of your site, you wouldn't need to put in the code because the browser will look for them there.

Finally, we added some startup images. These will be displayed while your web app is loading. The sizes we added accommodate the three variations of iPhones (regular, Retina, and iPhone 5) and both iPad screen types in landscape and portrait. It's important to rotate your landscape images 90 degrees clockwise (so they are in a vertical orientation) before saving them, so they will load correctly. We implemented these using a media query to display the correct image based on the devices' specifications and orientations.

There's more...

On the iPhone 5 you may find that your web app won't load in full screen. This issue is due to the `viewport` value of the `<meta>` tag. If you have a width set in this tag it will prevent the iPhone from properly scaling the app. Remove that setting and the issue should be resolved.

Scalable Vector Graphics (Become an expert)

Scalable Vector Graphics (**SVG**) are a great solution for creating high-definition images for your website. SVG images are an XML-based file format that use code to create graphics. Because SVGs are defined in XML they remain sharp at any size you scale them to. Additionally, they can be animated using **JavaScript** or **Synchronized Multimedia Integration Language** (**SMIL**). This provides a wide range of possibilities that aren't available in traditional images.

Vector graphics are best suited to images that are made up of easily definable shapes. These images could include icons, buttons, illustrations, and user-interface elements.

There are two methods to create an SVG. You can code it directly into an SVG or HTML file or you can create it using a compatible graphics editor. This recipe will show you how to create an SVG using both methods and display them in your browser.

Getting ready

To get started we'll need a graphics editor that works with SVG. If you have **Adobe Illustrator** or **CorelDRAW** you can use those applications to create an image and save it as an SVG. If you don't have one of these editors, I recommend using the open source editor **Inkscape** to create your SVG. You can download it for free at `http://inkscape.org/`.

How to do it...

1. First create a simple vector image within your graphics editor and save the file as `vector.svg` inside of your `/images/` folder within the `/retina/` folder.

2. Then create an HTML document called `svg.html` inside the `/retina/` folder. Inside the basic HTML structure, we'll embed the SVG graphic that we created in our image editor.

   ```
   <object data="images/vector.svg" type="image/svg+xml"></object>
   ```

3. Next we'll create a circle and a rectangle using SVG.

   ```
   <svg xmlns="http://www.w3.org/2000/svg" version="1.1">

     <circle cx="100" cy="300" r="100" stroke="black" stroke-
   width="1" fill="orange" />

     <rect x="300" y="200" width="200" height="200" fill="#009933" />

   </svg>
   ```

4. If you open the page within your browser you'll see the graphics we just added. Try zooming in or resizing the page to see how sharp they remain.

How it works...

The first SVG image that we created in our graphics program generated an XML-based file. If you'd like to, you can open it in your code editor and take a look at it. To add it to our page we used an object element. The object element is supported in all major browsers that display SVG images (Safari, Chrome, Firefox, IE 9+, Opera, and more). The disadvantage of this method is that it doesn't allow scripting in old versions of Internet Explorer.

If you'd like to use scripting with your SVG image you can use the `<embed>` tag. The embed tag (`<embed src="vector.svg" type="image/svg+xml" />`) still works with the same set of browsers, but if you're using an HTML4 or XHTML `doctype` at the beginning of your page it is invalid code. This code is allowed if you are using HTML5. More information on this topic is available at `http://www.w3.org/Graphics/SVG/IG/resources/svgprimer.html#SVG_in_HTML`.

Next we created some SVG shapes directly in our page. In most cases you'll want to have your SVG stored as a separate file, but this is a good way to see how the code works.

First, we added the SVG element and referenced its specification. Then we created a circle and defined the x-axis center (`cx`), the y-axis center (`cy`), the radius (`r`), `stroke`, `stroke-width`, and color (`fill`). The two axis values are not required, but they will help position the shape on your page.

Next we created a rectangle with some similar properties. The axis values (`x` and `y`) are based on the top-left corner of the rectangle unlike the circle, which is based on the center point. Notice that in the rectangle we used a hexadecimal value for the color. You can add colors by name, hex code, or RGB just like in CSS.

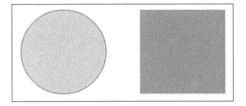

There's more...

SVG is not supported in some older browsers, primarily Internet Explorer (below Version 9). If you're concerned about supporting these browsers there are a few solutions available. You could detect support using Modernizr (`modernizr.com`), use Google Chrome Frame (`http://www.google.com/chromeframe?prefersystemlevel=true`), or use the Raphael JavaScript Library (`raphaeljs.com`).

Canvas (Become an expert)

Canvas is an HTML5 element that lets you create graphics using JavaScript. It is raster-based, which means that it has a set amount of pixels and is not updated when zooming, resulting in pixilation. Also, canvas is drawn using JavaScript so it is not accessible and will not work when JavaScript is disabled. This makes canvas a poor solution in most scenarios for creating Retina images.

In most cases it is recommended that you use another solution for creating high-density graphics, but we are going to cover canvas because there are some situations where you may want to use it. You may want to use canvas because it is often the best option for creating games or animated elements that require lots of data manipulation. These animations will typically run better in canvas than if you tried to use SVG.

This recipe will show the basics of the canvas element and show you how to create some simple shapes to get an idea of how canvas works.

How to do it...

1. To get started, create a new HTML document called `canvas.html` inside the `/retina/` folder. First, inside of the `<head>` tag of our HTML structure we'll add a call to include jQuery.

   ```
   <head>
     <script src="http://code.jquery.com/jquery-1.5.1.min.js"></
   script>
   </head>
   ```

2. Then inside of the `<body>` tag of our HTML we'll add a canvas element.

   ```
   <canvas id="myCanvas" width="400" height="400">
   </canvas>
   ```

3. Now that we have a canvas element, we can draw in it using JavaScript. First, we'll create variables for the values we'll need to change.

   ```
   <script type="text/javascript">

     var c = document.getElementById("myCanvas"),
       ratio = window.devicePixelRatio || 1,
       cWidth = c.width,
       cHeight = c.height,
       ctx = c.getContext('2d');
   ```

4. Then we'll add our code to change our variables if the device being used has a high-density display.

   ```
   if (ratio > 1) {
       $(c).attr('width', cWidth * window.devicePixelRatio);
   ```

```
$(c).attr('height', cHeight * window.devicePixelRatio);
$(c).css('width', cWidth);
$(c).css('height', cHeight);
ctx.scale(2, 2);
}
```

5. Now we'll start drawing some shapes onto our canvas element. First we'll draw a rectangle.

```
if (c.getContext) {
  var ctx = c.getContext('2d');
  ctx.fillStyle="#009820";
  ctx.fillRect(0,0,100,80);
```

6. Next we'll add a circle, continuing our `if` statement.

```
var ctx2 = c.getContext('2d');
ctx2.fillStyle="#cc0000";
ctx2.strokeStyle="#666666";
ctx2.arc(150,40,40,0,Math.PI*2,true);
ctx2.fill();
ctx2.stroke();
```

7. Then we'll add some text into our `if` statement.

```
var ctx3 = c.getContext('2d');
ctx3.shadowOffsetX = 1;
ctx3.shadowOffsetY = 1;
ctx3.shadowBlur = 2;
ctx3.shadowColor = "#999999";
ctx3.fillStyle="#000000";
ctx3.font="30px Helvetica";
ctx3.fillText("Canvas",200,30);

}
</script>
```

8. Now you can run this code inside your browser to see the graphics inside of our canvas.

How it works...

To begin we added the jQuery library to our code. This will make it easy to resize our canvas if the device is high-density. Then the first step to create our drawing was adding an HTML5 canvas element. We gave this element an `id` of `myCanvas`, so that we could manipulate it using JavaScript, and set its height and width.

Next we added some JavaScript code to draw within our canvas element. The first line of our script created a variable named c to reference the canvas element. Then we created variables to store the pixel ratio (to determine if the device is high-density) and the size of our canvas. Then we needed to create a variable to call the canvas element's getContext() method and set it to 2d so we can draw within the canvas.

Next we created an if statement to check if the devicePixelRatio value is greater than 1, meaning it is a Retina device. If this statement is true, we expand the HTML canvas size and then return it to the normal size in CSS. Then we set the scale of the context to be twice as large. This gives us double the amount of pixels within the same area.

Then we created another if statement to check if the user's browser supports canvas. By adding this you could choose an alternative for older browsers such as loading a static image in the canvas element's place.

Within our if statement we started by creating a rectangle. Using the context variable (ctx) that we created previously, we can start adding drawing methods and properties.

To start creating a rectangle we set the fillStyle property with the color we wanted it to be. Then we used fillRect to create a rectangle filled with that color. We added four values to this drawing method: x position, y position, width, and height. Now we have a green rectangle within our canvas.

Next, we added a circle to our canvas. To begin, we defined a new variable for a second context. This allows us to change the styles that will be applied to the shape. If we wanted the same style as our rectangle we could have continued to use the same context. We set a new fillStyle property and then added a strokeStyle property to set a dark grey stroke around our circle. Next we created a circle using arc(). The values we added to the arc specify the x position, y position, radius, start angle, end angle, and direction flag (true for counter-clockwise and false for clockwise). We used the Math module to calculate the radians for the circle. Then we applied our color fill and stroke to finish the circle.

Finally, we created some text in our canvas. To begin, we defined a third variable for this context. Then we added a shadow using similar settings to defining a drop-shadow in CSS. Then we set a fillStyle property (to color the text), a font size, and a font family. The last item in our if statement was fillText containing the text and x and y offsets.

There's more...

Canvas is an HTML5 element, which means that some older browsers do not support it. The main browser you'll need to watch out for is Internet Explorer (below Version 9). If you need support for older browsers you should include a fallback for your canvas.

Pixel ratio detection with JavaScript (Become an expert)

There are a number of good options for implementing Retina images with CSS and vector images, but there isn't a simple solution available for the standard <img> tag. Photographs and other images are typically added using HTML within the content of websites. Until we have a new HTML tag available or an update to the existing <img> tag to reference high-resolution images, we'll have to find an alternative solution.

Currently, the best two options available are using either a front-end or server-side scripting solution. This recipe will discuss how to use JavaScript to replace your normal images with high-resolution images if a Retina Display is detected.

Getting ready

To get started, we'll need a photo to use for our test page. If you've been following along with the previous recipes you can reuse your myImage.jpg photograph, or if not, any large photograph will work. I'll be using my original photo, which is 1400 x 800 pixels.

How to do it...

1. If you don't already have your photos saved from before, save your image as myImage@2x.jpg inside your /images/ folder within the /retina/ folder. Then resize the image to 50 percent and save it as myImage.jpg in the same folder.

2. Create an HTML document called javascript.html inside the /retina/ folder. Inside the <head> tag of the basic HTML structure, we'll start by including jQuery.

```
<head>

  <script src="http://code.jquery.com/jquery-1.5.1.min.js"></
script>

</head>
```

3. Next we'll add some HTML code to the `<body>` tag to display two versions of our photo.

```
<body>

    <img src="images/myImage.jpg" width="700" height="400" />

    <img src="images/myImage.jpg" class="retina" width="700"
height="400" />
```

4. Then we'll add some JavaScript to swap out the high-definition image.

```
<script type="text/javascript">
    $(function () {

        if (window.devicePixelRatio >= 2) {

            var images = $("img.retina"),
            imageType,
            imageName;

                // loop through the images and make them hi-res
            for(var i = 0; i < images.length; i++) {

                // create new image name
                imageType = images[i].src.substr(-4);
                imageName = images[i].src.substr(0, images[i].src.length
                - 4);
                imageName += "@2x" + imageType;

                //rename image
                images[i].src = imageName;

            }
        }

    });
    </script>
</body>
```

5. If you are working on a Retina device you should be able to open this page locally; if not, upload the folder to your web server and open the page on your device. You will notice how much sharper the second image is than the first image. On a device without a Retina Display, both images will look the same.

How it works...

To get started, we included the jQuery library to make it easy to select all the image elements on the page that we want to replace with high-resolution versions. This example is only replacing a single image, but the code can be applied to any images you add to your page.

Next, we added two HTML `<img>` tags. Make sure to specify the width and height of the images so when we replace the image with the Retina version the size remains the same. In the second `<img>` tag we included `class="retina"` because our JavaScript will use this class to determine which images to replace with a high-resolution version.

Then we created a JavaScript function to load our Retina images. Our script started with an `if` statement to check if the `window.devicePixelRatio` is equal to or greater than two, so we only run the script if the user is on a Retina device.

If a Retina device is being used, then we create three variables. The first variable, called `images`, is set to contain all the images with the `retina` class. Then we created two additional variables, `imageType` and `imageName`, to store the image's extension (for example, `.jpg`) and the filename without the extension.

The next section of code is a `for` loop, which continues to run until all the images with the `retina` class (that were stored in our `images` variable) have been updated. The first line of the loop sets `imageType` to the image's extension, which are the final four characters of the filename. Then it sets `imageName` to the initial part of the filename, without the extension. Now that we have the image name split into two variables, we're ready to add in our Retina image.

The next line of the loop adds `@2x` to the `imageName` property and then completes the filename by adding the extension. For this code to work, you'll need to name all your high-resolution images the same as your normal images, but add `@2x` at the end of the name like we've done here. Finally the `src` value of the `<img>` tag is set to our new high-resolution filename.

There's more...

When using this script you'll need to make sure to only add `class="retina"` to the images that you have supplied a high-resolution image for. If you add it to an image without a corresponding `@2x` image you'll have a broken `<img>` tag. You could also use this script without that class to simplify it, but you would have to be very careful to ensure that you have two versions of every image on your site.

There are a couple of downsides to this JavaScript based Retina image implementation. First, if the user has JavaScript disabled they will only see the regular images. Second, Retina browsers may begin to download the small images first before they are replaced, which may use extra bandwidth. This wouldn't be much of a concern on a small page with few images, but it could cause issues on larger sites.

Loading only the correct image

Making some changes to our code could solve the image loading issue (starting to load the small image before it has been replaced). Instead of setting `src` in our `<img>` tag, we could use `data-src` so the browser doesn't see the image location. Then in our JavaScript we would create a variable with the `data-src` attribute, set it to the image's `src` if the device is non-Retina, or add `@2x` and set that to `src` on a Retina device.

To make this work for browsers with JavaScript disabled, we'd also want to add our normal image tag wrapped inside of a `<noscript>` tag. You can download an implementation of this script called retinise from `dahliacreative.com/retinisejs` or try out Adam Bradley's `foresight.js` at `https://github.com/adamdbradley/foresight.js`. Adam's script also includes additional features, such as network connection testing to see if the user has a fast enough connection before loading the larger images.

Targeting other high-density devices

This script uses `window.devicePixelRatio >= 2` to detect Retina devices. All of Apple's Retina Displays have a pixel-ratio of `2`, which this code corresponds to, however other manufacturers may make displays with pixel-ratios below this value. If you'd like to target those devices as well, you could lower this value. For example, `window.devicePixelRatio >= 1.5`. This will depend on if you feel that it is worth serving the larger files to these devices, or you could create another `if` statement and corresponding images to target these devices specifically.

Server-side Retina solutions (Become an expert)

Instead of using JavaScript to display Retina images, you could implement a server-side Retina image solution. These solutions use JavaScript to determine if the user is on a Retina device and then use PHP to send a high-definition image instead of a normal one. The benefit of using one of these solutions is that the server automatically sends the correct version once the cookie is set, instead of needing to request it from the browser.

There are several open source solutions that have already been written to accomplish this task. In this recipe we will cover one such solution to see how it is implemented.

Getting ready

To get started, download Jeremy Worboys' **Retina Images** project at `http://retina-images.complexcompulsions.com/`. For this project to work you'll need a server that is running PHP. If you're using another language you may be able to find a similar script or use Jeremy's code as a reference to create your own solution.

We'll also need an image to test. You can use the `myImage.jpg` and `myImage@2x.jpg` images we used in earlier recipes. If you don't have these images use a large photo at 1400 x 800 pixels for `myImage@2x.jpg` and resize to 50 percent for `myImage.jpg`. Save them both inside the `images` folder within the `/retina/` folder.

How to do it...

1. Extract the files from the Retina Images project and add `retinaimages.php` and the `.htaccess` file to the root directory of your web server. If you already have an existing `.htaccess` file you'll want to add the new code to it rather than replacing it.

2. Create a new HTML document called `serverSide.html` inside the `/retina/` folder. Inside the `<head>` tag of our HTML structure we'll add some JavaScript to set a cookie.

```
<head>
  <script>
(function(w){
  var dpr=((w.devicePixelRatio===undefined)?1:w.devicePixelRatio);
  if(!!w.navigator.standalone){
    var r=new XMLHttpRequest();
    r.open('GET','/retinaimages.php?devicePixelRatio=' +
    dpr,false);
    r.send()
  } else {
    document.cookie='devicePixelRatio='+dpr+';
    path=/'
  }
})(window)
  </script>
</head>
```

3. Then inside the `<body>` tag of our HTML we'll add some CSS in case the user has JavaScript disabled.

```
<body>
  <noscript>
  <style id="devicePixelRatio" media="only screen and (-moz-min-
  device-pixel-ratio: 2), only screen and (-o-min-device-pixel-
  ratio: 2/1), only screen and (-webkit-min-device-pixel-ratio:
  2), only screen and (min-device-pixel-ratio: 2)">
  #devicePixelRatio {
    background-image:url("/retinaimages.php?devicePixelRatio=2")
  }
  </style>
  </noscript>
```

4. Then we'll add an image to test the code with.

```
<img src="images/myImage.jpg" width="700" height="400" />
</body>
```

5. Now you can open this page from your web server on your Retina device to test it out.

How it works...

Jeremy's code works by detecting the `devicePixelRatio` in JavaScript to determine if the user has a Retina Display. Then it sets a cookie with this data so that the PHP code can reference it. If the user has JavaScript disabled, the CSS code within the `<noscript>` tag creates a fallback reference. Make sure this code is above the stylesheets in your page so that any images that they contain are processed correctly after the cookie has been set.

We made sure to set the `height` and `width` attribute of the non-Retina image in our HTML `<img>` tag so that it is sized correctly when our high-definition image is served. You'll need to ensure this is set for all images and that CSS images have a `background-size` set. Any image you want served in high-definition will need to have the same filename as the original image with the addition of `@2x` as we've done here. They will also need to be in the same folder so the script can find them.

When the image is requested from the server the `.htaccess` file we added (or modified) will use the `retinaimages.php` file instead of serving it directly. This PHP code checks if the cookie for a Retina device is set and that there is an `@2x` version of the image. If these are both true, the high-definition image will be served. If it is not true, then the regular version is served.

Thank you for buying
Instant Website Optimization for Retina Displays How-to

About Packt Publishing

Packt, pronounced 'packed', published its first book "*Mastering phpMyAdmin for Effective MySQL Management*" in April 2004 and subsequently continued to specialize in publishing highly focused books on specific technologies and solutions.

Our books and publications share the experiences of your fellow IT professionals in adapting and customizing today's systems, applications, and frameworks. Our solution based books give you the knowledge and power to customize the software and technologies you're using to get the job done. Packt books are more specific and less general than the IT books you have seen in the past. Our unique business model allows us to bring you more focused information, giving you more of what you need to know, and less of what you don't.

Packt is a modern, yet unique publishing company, which focuses on producing quality, cutting-edge books for communities of developers, administrators, and newbies alike. For more information, please visit our website: www.packtpub.com.

Writing for Packt

We welcome all inquiries from people who are interested in authoring. Book proposals should be sent to author@packtpub.com. If your book idea is still at an early stage and you would like to discuss it first before writing a formal book proposal, contact us; one of our commissioning editors will get in touch with you.

We're not just looking for published authors; if you have strong technical skills but no writing experience, our experienced editors can help you develop a writing career, or simply get some additional reward for your expertise.

iOS 5 Essentials

ISBN: 978-1-84969-226-7   Paperback: 252 pages

Harness iOS 5's new powerful features to create stunning applications

1. Integrate iCloud, Twitter and AirPlay into your applications.

2. Lots of step-by-step examples, images and diagrams to get you up to speed in no time with helpful hints along the way.

3. Each chapter explains iOS 5's new features in-depth, whilst providing you with enough practical examples to help incorporate these features in your apps

4. From the author of Xcode 4 iOS development.

HTML5 Canvas Cookbook

ISBN: 978-1-84969-136-9   Paperback: 348 pages

Over 80 recipes to revolutionize the web experience with HTML5 Canvas

1. The quickest way to get up to speed with HTML5 Canvas application and game development

2. Create stunning 3D visualizations and games without Flash

3. Written in a modern, unobtrusive, and objected oriented JavaScript style so that the code can be reused in your own applications.

4. Part of Packt's Cookbook series: Each recipe is a carefully organized sequence of instructions to complete the task as efficiently as possible

Please check **www.PacktPub.com** for information on our titles

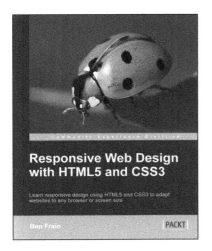

Responsive Web Design with HTML5 and CSS3

ISBN: 978-1-84969-318-9   Paperback: 324 pages

Learn responsive design using HTML5 and CSS3 to adapt websites to any browser or screen size

1. Everything needed to code websites in HTML5 and CSS3 that are responsive to every device or screen size

2. Learn the main new features of HTML5 and use CSS3's stunning new capabilities including animations, transitions and transformations

3. Real world examples show how to progressively enhance a responsive design while providing fall backs for older browsers

HTML5 Mobile Development Cookbook

ISBN: 978-1-84969-196-3   Paperback: 254 pages

Over 60 recipes for building fast, responsive HTML5 mobile websites for iPhone 5, Android, Windows Phone, and Blackberry

1. Solve your cross platform development issues by implementing device and content adaptation recipes.

2. Maximum action, minimum theory allowing you to dive straight into HTML5 mobile web development.

3. Incorporate HTML5-rich media and geo-location into your mobile websites.

Please check **www.PacktPub.com** for information on our titles